OREGON

Photography by Steve Terrill

Oregon

Photography by Steve Terrill

ISBN-13 978-1-60068-259-9

First Printing, December 2008

4961 Windplay Drive, El Dorado Hills, CA 95762
www.impactphotographics.com

Printed in China

In the lower elevation of Oregon's Cascade Mountains lies a temperate rain forest in Silver Falls State Park. The Lower South Falls cascades 177 feet to a forest floor covered with ferns, mosses, and wildflowers.

An unmarred blanket of fall leaves only serve to enhance the beauty of this neighborhood in Portland.

Officially named Tom McCall Waterfront Park, but known to Oregonians as just Waterfront Park, this is often the center of activity in Portland. Waterfront Park is located on the west bank of the Willamette River in downtown Portland, where the city skyline is seen jutting out in the background.

The stunning colors of sunset touch the top of Heceta Head Lighthouse, located on a bluff 150 feet above the ocean. It is the most powerful lighthouse along the Oregon coast where its light can be seen 21 miles out to sea.

Lush farmland fed by a full winding stream is undeniably beautiful with the snow-capped Wallowa Mountains serving as the perfect backdrop. The Wallowa Mountains are a mountain range located in the Columbia Plateau of northeastern Oregon. The range runs approximately 40 miles.

Storm clouds break to reveal a stunning rainbow next to The Crown Point Vista House, built in 1916. Crown Point is a land mass peninsula on the Columbia River Gorge, located in eastern Multnomah County, approximately 15 miles east of Portland.

Clear skies from the top of The Crown Point Vista House allow an unobstructed view of Portland only 15 miles to the west. It also offers a spectacular look at the Columbia River below from its stately position atop Crown Point.

The landscape is picturesque below the Strawberry Mountains in John Day River Valley. Remnants of an old barn and corral sit adjacent to world famous fossil beds that are closely tied to the uniquely layered features of the sprawling area.

Famous for its deep blue color and impressive water clarity, Crater Lake is the central feature of Crater Lake National Park. Crater Lake is a caldera lake, a volcanic feature formed by the collapse of land following a volcanic eruption.

The various foliage surrounding Middle North Falls in Oregon's Silver Falls State Park, the largest state park in Oregon, includes Douglas Fir, Hemlock, and Cedar. The double tiered waterfall has an amphitheater-like surrounding where you can walk behind the falls and feel the misty spray.

Smooth waters mirror a row of houseboats on the Columbia River in northeast Portland.

Numerous boats sit on the glassy water atop their perfect reflections at dusk along the Columbia River Channel at Tomahawk Island in Portland.

Forty-plus miles of the central Oregon coast are home to the Oregon Dunes National Recreation Area. Here, majestic sand dunes hundreds of feet high provide a habitat for forests, rivers, wetlands, and wildlife. Recreational opportunities abound for hikers, nature-lovers, photographers and off-road vehicle enthusiasts. Among the features of the NRA are 30 lakes for fishing, swimming and wildlife watching, 14 hiking trails through wetlands, forests and dunes, numerous campgrounds and day use areas.

The solitude of the Chalk Basin Formations in the lower Owyhee Canyon Wilderness Study Area, in Malheur County, Oregon is emphasized by the depth of the canyon combined with its limited view around and beyond the staggering peak formations.

With rocky cliffs and tempestuous waves that beat them, the necessity of lighthouses is obvious. Off in the distance, Cape Arago or Gregory Light Station as noted in early light lists, was the first lighthouse constructed after Oregon became a state in 1859. The actual islet the lighthouse station is situated on is also known as "Chief's Island" and "Lighthouse Island." Cape Arago's tower is 44 feet high and was illuminated in 1934.

Shore Acres State Park is an Oregon State Park located on the Cape Arago Highway south of Coos Bay. The park has five acres of formal gardens that literally burst with color year round.

An Indian Burial Canoe is propped up near the Astoria Column, a tower overlooking the mouth of the Columbia River on Coxcomb Hill in Astoria, Oregon. The 125-foot-tall column was built in 1926 and served for over 80 years as a beacon on the Pacific Northwest Coast. It sits in a wooded area 600 feet above sea level.

The sunrise shines through trees heavy laden with fresh snow along Still Creek in Mt. Hood National Forest.

Oregon Caves National Monument in the Siskiyou Mountains, southwestern Oregon, is known primarily for its marble caves. The Oregon Caves Chateau is a historic American hotel that opened in 1934. The Chateau is six stories high and is built across a steep ravine.

Pioneer Courthouse Square, affectionately known as Portland's living room, is a public space occupying a full 40,000 square feet of a city block in the center of downtown Portland. The square is named after the Pioneer Courthouse, an 1875 federal building occupying the block directly east of the square. The Square is one of Portland's leading outdoor venues, hosting over 300 events each year that range from large-scale concerts to cultural festivals, such as the Festival of Flowers held annually.

The immaculate grounds of Washington Park in Portland serve as the ultimate forefront to the city's skyline. Clear skies expand the horizon with a clear view of Mt. Hood in the background.

Baker Beach near Florence, Oregon is stunning as its sand dunes reflect the morning light creating a distinct separation from the waters of the Pacific Ocean.

Wallowa Lake, with Bonneville Mountain sitting in the background, stretches for 5 miles. A perfect morainal lake, which means it was formed by a glacier, is surrounded on three sides by 9,000 foot tall snow-capped mountains and beautiful foliage.

The impending sunset heightens the colors of the sky and Mt. Hood's reflection in the water inside Mt. Hood National Forest.

Crater Lake is located in Southern Oregon on the crest of the Cascade Mountain range, 100 miles east of the Pacific Ocean, and is surrounded by sheer cliffs almost two thousand feet high. It is a place of immeasurable beauty, including two picturesque islands that stand in contrast covered in snow against the deep sapphire blue water.

A small portion of the North Umpqua River is channeled into a narrow gorge, where it drops down several small falls before hurling over a pair of basalt cliffs. The upper fall drops 28 feet and the lower 85 feet into an aqua blue pool. With a reliable water flow on the North Umpqua River, the Toketee, a Chinook Indian name meaning "graceful," avoids the seasonal fluctuations of other creek-fed waterfalls in Oregon.

Crab traps and floats stacked on the shore across from docked boats at Yaquina Bay in Newport show the diversified use of water on the northwestern shore of Oregon's coastal waters.

The sunrise streaks the sky over Coos Bay, the largest city on the Oregon coast. Coos Bay is part of Oregon's Bay Area and has the largest natural harbor between Seattle and San Francisco, making it a major shipping and manufacturing center.

Haystack Rock and the Needles appear to just float above the water in Oregon's Coastal National Wildlife Refuge at Cannon Beach.

Smith Rock State Park is located in central Oregon. Its sheer cliffs are magnificant and accentuated in a late winter snowfall. Smith Rock is generally considered the birthplace of modern American sport climbing.

The Columbia River Gorge is a spectacular river canyon cutting the only sea-level route through the Cascade Mountain Range. The Old Columbia River Highway runs along the Gorge path, twisting and turning with views of the river, dotted with colors that vary depending on the season, and breathtaking waterfalls.

Mt. Hood is mirrored in the pristine waters of Trillium Lake just southwest of the mountain.

Touched with fresh snow, Wizard's Island sitting in solitude in the middle of Crater Lake, also known as the "Witches Cauldron," appears deceptively small in its isolation.

Pumice and Scoria pinnacles jut out of the ground at Crater Lake National Park in Southern Oregon. The peaks' staggering height only serve to magnify their stature.

Fall colors frame Multnomah Falls as it feeds into the Columbia River Gorge.

The pink of a Rhododendron bush is intensified in contrast to the pale sand as it clings to a slope near Florence in Oregon Dunes National Recreation Area.

The John Day Fossil Beds National Monument in Eastern Oregon is world-renowned for its well-preserved, remarkably complete record of fossil plants and animals. The Blue Basin, inside the park, is composed of claystones that are the decomposed remnants of volcanic ash.

A late winter snowfall leaves a pristine layer of snow surrounding the South Falls in Silver Falls State Park.

Winter snow adds to the beauty of the view as seen from the Crown Point Vista House, built in 1916.

A stunning natural basalt arch in the Columbia River Gorge National Scenic Area is as a natural frame to St. Peters Dome in the distance.

One of the most photographed bridges in Oregon, the Goodpasture Covered Bridge is also the second longest covered bridge in the state. The structure has superb architectural detailing; specifically, 10 gothic style louvered windows on each side.

The Strawberry Mountain Wilderness is a mix of rugged alpine ridges and peaks that overlook beautiful meadows and glacial lakes. The late summer is met with lingering snow against the rocky basins.

The rushing waters of Multnomah Falls push through a late winter snowfall.

The Port of Portland sits on the banks of the Willamette River and works not only as an industrial waterfront, but is home to unique shops found only along the cobblestone streets of the port.

Boats bask in the light of sunset on the Columbia River Channel at Hayden Island, an island in the Columbia River between Vancouver, Washington and Portland, Oregon, where even Mt. Hood can be seen in the distance.

Rock formations in Smith Rock State Park are a sanctuary of majestic rock spires overlooking the scenic Crooked River Canyon. This park has international recognition for its rock climbing opportunities and draws visitors from around the world.

Laurelhurst Park is a perfect example of the City Beautiful Movement in landscaping. In 1919, the park was named the most beautiful park on the west coast by the Pacific Coast Parks Association. In February 2001, Laurelhurst Park was named to the National Register of Historic Places, the first city park ever listed on the national register.

Spectacular sweeps of Beargrass and Rhododendrons at LoLo Pass during warmer weather are in a valley at the base of snow covered Mt. Hood.

In the Columbia River Gorge National Scenic Area in northern Oregon can be seen the second highest year-round waterfall in the nation. Plummeting 620 feet from its origins on Larch Mountain is Multnomah Falls. At the base of the falls lays the historic Multnomah Falls Lodge, built in 1925.

Hood River, Oregon is a Columbia River Gorge town famed for its windsurfing. The Columbia Gorge Hotel was originally developed in 1904 where it has remained in its stately condition ever since, sitting next to the beautiful waters of the river.

Washington County, Oregon is centered on a fertile plain that attracted farmers before the first wagon trains ever traveled through. In 1997, orchards covered 8,403 acres of the county's lands and 1,163 acres were devoted to vineyards.

The Willamette Valley, Oregon's leading wine region, stretches for more than a hundred miles, buffered from Pacific storms on the west by the Coast Range to the Willamette River on the north in Yamhill County.

At the height of the Great Depression in 1936, ground was broken for the Timberline Lodge on Mt. Hood where it sits at approximately 6,000 feet. Virtually sitting in the clouds, the lodge's impressive stonework, woodwork, and art collections are only enhanced by its incredible locale.

Peninsula Park Rose Garden is located in north Portland. This two acre sunken rose garden is packed with over 10,000 traditional rose plantings surrounded by sweeping arches and creatively designed, lush paths. The octagonal bandstand was constructed in 1913. It was used for World War I patriotic demonstrations and is now the site for many weddings and concerts.

In the forefront, a juniper tree is touched by the sunrise with Mt. Jefferson, the second highest peak in Oregon, peaking over the ridge in the background of Lake Billy Chinook, Jefferson County.

Located in Wheeler County, Oregon, the Painted Hills span 3,132 acres. Named after the colorful layers of its hills, this ancient river floodplain shows the distinct various geological eras in its stripes.

On the southern Oregon coast with sand dunes and a brilliantly colored landscape is Pistol River State Park. The dunes and the river system that feed them are what make this area unique. During the spring and summer months, the dunes actually grow. The river has changed its course numerous times in recent history and pothole ponds attract waterfowl and shorebirds. The river supposedly got its name when a militia soldier lost his pistol in the river during the infamous Rogue River Indian War in March of 1856, when the decisive battle was fought here.

The Taft Rocks and a Great Blue Heron are silhouetted at sunset in Siletz, Lincoln County. Siletz Bay National Wildlife Refuge consists of some of the most scenic aquatic habitat along the Oregon Coast National Scenic Byway.

The Deschutes National Forest comprises 1.8 million acres along the eastern side of the Cascade Mountains. A rustic corral in Sparks Lake Meadow within the national forest sits below Mt. Bachelor, evidence of the rich human and natural history here.

"Faith," "Hope," and "Charity"… were the names given to the Three Sisters volcanic peaks of the Cascade Volcanic Arc and the Cascade Range by early settlers in Oregon. They're undeniably spectacular, each exceeding 10,000 feet in elevation.

The Kiger Mustangs are thought to be one of the most pure herds of Spanish Mustangs existing in the wild today. Kiger possess the qualities of endurance, and the cunning ability to survive not only the harshest elements of nature but the most relentless pursuits of mankind.

Upper Klamath Lake in Upper Klamath National Wildlife Refuge is a large, shallow freshwater lake east of the Cascade Range in south central Oregon. It is approximately 20 miles long and 8 miles wide and extends northwest from the city of Klamath Falls, and is the largest freshwater body in Oregon. The smooth, pristine waters magnify the colors of sunset in its reflection.